Everything You Need to Know About *Falling in Love*

A happy young couple stare at each other in loving admiration.

Everything You Need to Know About Falling in Love

Lauren Spencer

The Rosen Publishing Group, Inc.
New York

To DJ, who unveils a new definition of love to me every day, making my life a lovely place to be

Published in 2001 by The Rosen Publishing Group, Inc.
29 East 21st Street, New York, NY 10010

Library of Congress Cataloging-in-Publication Data

Spencer, Lauren.
Everything you need to know about falling in love / by Lauren Spencer.— 1st ed.
p. cm. — (The need to know library)
Includes bibliographical references and index.
ISBN 0-8239-3395-4 (lib. bdg.)
1. Love—Juvenile literature. 2. Adolescent psychology—Juvenile literature. 3. Teenagers—Attitudes—Juvenile literature. 4. Interpersonal relations—Juvenile literature. [1. Love. 2. Interpersonal relations.]
I. Title. II. Series.
HQ801 .S685 2001
306.7—dc21

2001000754

Manufactured in the United States of America

Contents

Introduction

*T*he moment I saw him behind the counter in the cafeteria, I couldn't take my eyes off him. I don't know what it was, but he just looked cool. Suddenly, I felt really nervous and lost my appetite, which was crazy since I'd been starving right before then. I almost turned around and left the lunchroom. I was sure that my friend Patti could tell I was freaking out, but she just kept on talking.

Once we got to the front of the line, I couldn't even look at him. When I finally did manage to ask for a Coke, my voice sounded really funny and squeaky. He gave it to me without even looking up and I went to the cashier feeling stupid. The whole thing probably lasted about five minutes, but it felt like a lifetime and my heart was beating like a drum. It was pretty painful.

In this scene from the 1999 movie American Pie, *Heather (Mena Suvari) stares at Oz (Chris Klein) in wide-eyed infatuation.*

Affairs of the Heart

Romantic love is often dramatic and overwhelming. Although falling in love can feel as warm and comfortable as putting on a favorite sweater, it can also send you on a personal roller-coaster ride. Your heart, the organ primarily responsible for pumping blood through your body, also measures these emotional fluctuations. It takes your emotional temperature and registers when something extraordinary is happening by quickening its beats. So it's certainly no surprise that when something as exciting as falling in love occurs, your heart responds.

Although the heart is a popular symbol of love, studies show that the brain responds most intensely to love, sending the first physical messages through a series of chemical releases. Those first moments of elation, followed by infatuation, are brought about when a portion of the brain releases natural amphetamines. These amphetamines stimulate, or quicken, your heartbeat.

After spending time with the object of your desire, that initial rush will subside and your brain will release neurochemicals known as endorphins. These neurochemicals reduce sensations of pain and affect emotions. They help you feel safe and at peace in the company of your beloved.

Other Physical Reactions

Your body experiences other physical sensations when you are smitten. You may lose your appetite, have trouble falling asleep, or feel breathless. In fact, love is often characterized as a fever. While these may not sound like particularly enjoyable sensations, when combined with the high of falling in love, these feelings often result more from pleasure than pain.

Day after day I saw him working in the cafeteria, but I never had the nerve to say anything to him. I'd think about him all the time. While getting dressed in the morning, I'd practice little things I hoped to say to him. Once I got to school, I never said anything.

Honestly, sometimes I didn't recognize myself. I was no longer the happy-go-lucky person I had been only weeks earlier. It was one of the most uncomfortable things I've ever felt. It was wonderful, too. One day, about two weeks after I'd first seen him, he looked up and said, "Hi." I almost passed out.

Chapter 1

Notions of Love

Although it is often said that love is timeless, socially accepted ways of expressing romantic love have changed over time. You have probably read about the joys and tragedies of love in literature classes. The creation stories of many cultures also explore love and its special powers.

Ancient Western myths often characterize the search for love as the search for one's soulmate—one's other half. In fact, the driving force in some ancient myths is the hero's search for his or her soulmate. Once united with this love, he or she becomes figuratively whole.

Eros

In Greek mythology, Aphrodite (known as Venus in Roman mythology) is the goddess of love and beauty. Countless stories depict her capacity for joy and her

This sixteenth-century painting depicts Cupid in the act of shooting one of his love-inducing arrows.

loveliness, but they also record her destructive side. She was a goddess who understood that love can bring both pleasure and pain.

Eros (or Cupid in Roman mythology) was Aphrodite's son. He possessed arrows that enabled him to induce love between mortals and even between gods. Artists often depict Eros wearing a blindfold, because love is said to be blind. In fact, Eros himself was not immune to love. He fell for a mortal maiden named Psyche (Greek for "soul").

The story of Eros and Psyche illustrates one of the ways ancient Greek mythology defined love. Aphrodite despised Psyche. She was jealous of Psyche's beauty and humility. Because Eros was so deeply in love with Psyche, he ignored his mother's feelings. Instead, Eros elevated his beloved to the status of goddess and married her. In this way, Greek mythology united love and soul forever. This concept of love, often understood as "eros," centers on the romantic and spiritual union of two individuals.

Agape

Contrasting eros is a broader notion of love known as agape. "Agape" is a Greek word most notably invoked in the Christian Bible. Agape describes the love of God for humanity, as well as human worship of God. In the early history of Christianity, religious elders hosted agapes, or love feasts, bringing together both rich and poor to share bread and wine. Over time, this concept of love also referred to love of one's fellow man or woman, not in a romantic sense, but in a more global and humanitarian way.

Courtly Love

Expressions of romantic love in Europe did not become well documented until the twelfth century, during the feudal era. Wealth was concentrated in the hands of the very few. Most people toiled as peasants, working the land; their lives centered on the struggle to survive. Although minstrels sang love's praises and poets recited its virtues, their compositions focused primarily on people of wealth, the ruling class. As cities developed, social life revolved more and more around emotional dramas within the royal court.

Courtly love describes a very strict code of conduct for lovers that developed in medieval Europe. In stories about this era, knights were expected to fight for the hands and hearts of fair maidens, princesses, and queens. Ideally, they had already fallen head over heels in love with each other at first sight. They would then spend hours in agony, waiting for a glance from their beloveds to set their feelings ablaze.

Often ladies were already married or were engaged to someone else, but these were loveless unions. Marriages represented a business contract between two families and frequently involved the acquisition of land and wealth. As a result, a married woman might continue to hope that true or romantic love would find her someday.

True love usually arrived in the form of a gallant knight, who would prove himself worthy of a lady by fighting for her honor. These battles tested a young man's courage and valor. Although the women never engaged in warfare themselves, they were more than mere prizes. They were the driving force behind their lovers' every move. Their intelligence and beauty commanded a great deal of respect.

Courtly love's powerful message of chivalry has lasted in one form or another to this day. We still often

Prince Henry (Dougray Scott) falls in love with penniless Danielle (Drew Barrymore) in the movie Ever After, a modern spin on the classic Cinderella tale.

revel in true and imagined stories of lovers fighting overwhelming odds to hold onto one another. Although these dramatic stories are compelling, there is more to true love than drama.

Into the Modern Age

In the eighteenth century, love between two people required more one-to-one communication. Courtly love gave way to courting, when young men and women committed themselves only to each other. Although the terms people employed to discuss love in the eighteenth century differ from contemporary lingo, the romantic stages they described persist. For instance, the eighteenth-century practice of courting was known as "going steady" in the 1950s. Today, it's all about "hooking up."

In the eighteenth century, the term "courtship" referred to the period in a relationship before a couple married. Today, we often refer to this period as an engagement. In the past, people may have said they were "struck with love" when they had a crush or an infatuation. The eighteenth-century practice of "bundling"—when two people who were courting slept together fully clothed——might now be understood as "petting" or "making out," minus the overnight stay.

Living in the twentieth century, you may feel that you have more freedom to decide whom you choose to fall in love with, who makes the first move, and how

Freaks and Geeks *is one of many television series that portrays the loves and lives of American high school students.*

you express yourself in that love. Along with those choices though, comes more responsibility. It also creates a great deal of pressure—pressure to grow up and experience forms and expressions of love faster than ever before.

Although it may seem like everyone around you is obsessed with finding love, you need not rush into a relationship. What you might first think is love may actually be a passing infatuation. Ideally, when love is real, you feel it naturally. It will also provide you with a chance to develop and explore another part of yourself.

Chapter 2

Is This Love?

I'm usually really levelheaded. I think things through and I wouldn't normally put up with a long-distance relationship. But this guy, Chad, is worth it. I just knew that if I was willing to think about someone who lives 5,000 miles away, he must be special. At first it was crazy. I'd have $300 to $400 phone bills. My father would yell at me and look over every call on the bill saying, "Three hundred minutes? What could you possibly talk about for that long?" I was furious with my dad for not understanding. Also, I was working and paying the phone bills, so I didn't think it was my dad's business. I knew that Chad and I had plenty to talk about. We could talk forever.

Teens in love often get in trouble with their parents for spending too much time on the telephone.

Figuring It Out

Whether it's the first time or the one hundredth, when you talk to someone you really like, your heart beats loudly and you feel nervous. Infatuations, crushes, and puppy love can cause you to obsess about another person. You may feel that you want to spend all of your time with him or her. You think this person is special. How do you know whether your feelings will last? What if it turns out to be a passing phase? If the person you are interested in returns your affections, then you will have a chance to find out if these feelings will lead to love.

Flirting

The way he looked at me while we stood there talking made me feel really special. It was like there was nobody else at the party but me. He was laughing at all of my jokes and even blushing a little bit. I was blown away and thought, "Man, this guy is really cool." It wasn't like I was learning a lot about him as much as feeling that he was giving off this great energy.

When my friend came up and interrupted the conversation, I got really annoyed. Then I noticed that my crush was treating him the same way, laughing and teasing. Then it dawned on me that this guy was a major flirt. I got a little mad because I really thought that he was somebody I might like to go out with, but after watching the way he worked the room, I decided to look for someone else to talk to, someone a little more real.

Flirting pertains to a certain way of talking and acting. Some say flirting is an art. It can also simply be a good way to meet new people. Certainly, some people are more comfortable with the act of flirting than are others.

Sometimes flirting is viewed as a bad thing. People might say someone is a tease if all he or she does is flirt. If someone flirts constantly, other people may not trust that he or she is capable of, or interested, in

It is often difficult to tell whether someone who flirts with you at a party is really interested in getting to know you.

having a monogamous (exclusive) relationship. On the other hand, flirting can also be a great way to build self-confidence. Learning how to approach and talk to someone you find attractive can be fun. Flirting also enables you to engage in a conversation without becoming instantly attached or vulnerable.

A Crush

You can have a crush on someone you know or on a perfect stranger—someone you see performing music onstage or acting on a movie screen. Regardless of who the object of your desire is, a crush can completely take over your every waking moment. You may

Performing artists, like 'N Sync, are often the objects of teenage crushes.

find yourself thinking about the person constantly. If you know or see the person around a lot, you may feel tongue-tied and nervous in his or her presence.

In fact, you may have no interest in getting to know the person. Communicating with someone you have a crush on can be intimidating, so you may choose to admire him or her from a distance. Not telling anyone about these emotions can leave you feeling lonely. At the same time, knowing that the crush remains private can be comforting. In this way, you are not taking any chances or opening yourself up to rejection.

"A crush is when you're really shy around someone. You share your thoughts with your friends, saying, 'I like him (or her), but don't tell anyone,'" Debbie, a self-professed queen of crushes, explains. "Puppy love is when you are so satisfied that you can keep it to yourself. You don't necessarily want to share it with anyone. Plus, you can see his or her flaws without freaking out. In crushes, you usually ignore flaws, but with puppy love it's that middle stage where you can accept his or her flaws and even be willing to let the person know about your feelings."

Puppy Love

Puppy love usually describes the initial, blissful state of a relationship. After two people have acknowledged

It can be comforting to admit having a crush on someone to your friends, or you may choose to keep your feelings to yourself.

their interest in each other, they freely express the excitement and attraction they share. Unfortunately, arriving at this point involves taking a certain amount of risk. Admitting your attraction to someone may cause you to feel nervous and vulnerable. If you find out that he or she returns your interest, you will probably experience a sense of relief and elation. As the two of you become closer, these feelings of intense joy can sometimes mingle with jealousy and possessiveness.

On the other hand, you may choose to hide your true feelings for a while, just until you are sure that the other person feels the same way about you. Slowly, you may begin to share your inner thoughts with and trust one another. Soon you may both acknowledge what you mean to each other. Remember that it's up to you to choose when and how you want to express your romantic interest.

Tips for Approaching Someone You Like

◎ Find out whether you have any common interest with the person.

◎ If you are in the same class or extra-curricular group, start a conversation about it.

◎ Be bold and confident; believe in your power to be interesting.

◎ Look the person in the eye and speak clearly.

◎ If he or she seems distracted or you are incredibly uncomfortable, end the conversation as gracefully as possible.

When Friendship Becomes Love

I had known this girl since my first year of high school and all of a sudden when we came back to school after summer break, I decided that I was in love with her. It was weird; I felt as though I'd

never seen her before. I was asking everyone, "What should I do?" I was really scared that it would ruin our friendship.

Finally, I was sitting there doing homework, telling myself that I'm such a scaredy-cat and that she's a really nice girl. I know she won't be mean about it. So I decided to call her and tell her how I felt. I was giving myself a pep talk and everything. I finally called her. I was sweating bullets and talking about all this strange stuff, then finally I said, "Look, I've got to tell you something and if you start acting funny around me once I tell you, then I'll freak." She said, "Why would I act funny around you?"

Once I told her how I felt, she said that she wasn't really into me like that and she really just wanted to stay friends. Even though at the time I shrugged it off and made it seem like it was fine, I did feel weird when I hung up the phone. I was kind of worried about how she'd act when we saw each other at school.

Of course, she did start acting funny, but we managed to get back to normal and be friends again. In the end, I was actually glad that I got up the courage to tell her because it kind of made us closer. I guess I was lucky because it doesn't always turn out that way.

Sometimes, close friendships blossom into romantic relationships.

When you are close friends with someone, you may find yourself suddenly drawn to him or her in a romantic way. Some people worry that if friendship crosses the line into love and it doesn't work out, the friendship will be forever lost. Friendships can also become strained if one friend feels strongly for the other but is afraid that revealing his or her feelings will ruin the friendship. Although the transition can prove complicated, friendship can provide a solid foundation on which to build a romantic relationship. As friends, you have established your ability to communicate with each other and are comfortable sharing your hopes and fears.

Same-Sex Love

I had been struggling all year with the fact that I knew I was gay. I didn't know whom to tell, and all of these confusing feelings were rising inside of me. His name was Jason and I was sure that he would figure out that I liked him more than just wanting to be his friend.

I was afraid that someone would notice that I was acting weird and tell everyone. Jason was a grade ahead of me, so I didn't see him in classes or the gym, but I would go to track meets. Sometimes I made up excuses so I could stick around after school and wander by practice just to see him. He was tall and thin and ran really fast.

I knew he had a girlfriend and I knew that I could never tell him how I really felt. A lot of people admired him. He was really popular, so I don't think he suspected anything different about my attention. He probably didn't even notice me, except in the hall when I would go by his locker in the morning and say, "Hi."

Then Jason's dad got a job in another state and they moved away when I was in tenth grade. I never saw him again. I was devastated, and what made it so much worse was not having anyone to talk to about it. Slowly, I've been able to

A lesbian couple share a kiss on the Mall during the fourth annual national march for gay, lesbian, bisexual, and transgender rights in Washington, DC on April 30, 2000.

find other people to talk to about being gay and falling in love. It really helps. I don't feel quite as frustrated and lonely as I used to.

Although social tolerance of gay and lesbian relationships has slowly and steadily increased, homophobia persists. For this reason, being gay and falling in love can create special challenges. Accepting how you feel can take time. Add to that the emotional upheaval that can accompany falling in love, and the fear might hinder your desire to pursue a relationship.

Even today, as more and more people become comfortable with different lifestyles, coming out and being openly gay in school can be intimidating. Rather than live in the shadows pretending you're someone you're not, or keeping your feelings bottled up inside of you, you might think about finding people to talk to. Support groups offer suggestions and approaches to coming out, as well as a safe place to share your feelings and socialize.

To Whom Can You Turn?

◎ **Find an adult—a parent, teacher, or counselor—whom you trust. Tell that person how you feel and ask him or her for advice and support-group referrals.**

Many gay teenagers agonize about coming out to their parents. If you feel uncomfortable approaching a parent, perhaps consult a trusted friend or counselor.

◎ Be clear and positive about your identity and remember that you will eventually meet other gay and lesbian teens, and find safe spaces in which to express yourself.

First Love

When love hits, it can feel all-consuming, like being caught in a whirlwind. You feel like you want to know everything about the person you love. You learn new things about each other every day. You realize that you have tons of things in common. You share special songs, important places, and precious memories. You become best friends.

At times, you may both feel like you're being swept away into something larger than either one of you. Loving someone often entails hoping for a future together. It can also involve worrying that the object of your affection may not feel as strongly as you do.

Like many types of relationships, romantic ones involve a certain level of work and commitment. You may need to talk out disagreements, discuss insecurities, and decide to what extent you can deal with each other's faults. Nevertheless, first love is a unique and unforgettable experience.

Chapter 3

The Real Thing

It is more than just a passing moment. You have committed yourself heart and soul to another person. You feel all the twists and turns that falling in love brings. You share special memories with each other, certain songs and places remind you of each other. A warm, wonderful feeling comes over you when you think of your love. You find yourself daydreaming about the other person when he or she is not there. You feel unusually distracted, but it's all good. Although you may not care all that much about what the rest of the world thinks, there are people in your world who care about you.

Parents

My dad runs a business from his house and there's this young guy, Mark, who works with

When you fall in love, you may find yourself frequently distracted and daydreaming a lot.

him. I've liked him for about a year. At first we would only flirt with each other. Then, a few months ago, he asked me on a date. I was really nervous because I knew my dad wouldn't like me seeing him. This guy just isn't the type Dad would want me to go out with. In fact, my dad doesn't want me to go out with any guys at all. Last year, my dad had picked up on the fact that this guy liked me, but I told him not to worry about it.

Now, we're in love. It's sweet when Mark's over at the house and he's trying to get my attention. I don't know where it will go from here because I'm not sure my dad will ever

understand. In fact, one day when Mark was over, my dad said, "You should go downstairs and talk to him because I want you to see what kind of a knucklehead he is."

Regardless of the situation, introducing your new love to your parents, and meeting his or hers, can be a nerve-wracking experience. Parents can sometimes seem tough and strict when it comes to dating and affairs of the heart, but they can also be a good source of support and caring. Talking to them about someone special in your life also lets them know that you are expanding your world, making important choices, and becoming more independent.

> *Shayla told me that her parents had never liked the people she'd dated, so I was instantly freaked out. But our first meeting turned out better than I had expected. Her mom pulled out all the family photo albums with her baby pictures and her dad started discussing poetry with me because he knew I was into English literature. I was expecting her parents to be really intimidating, but they turned out to be very sweet. Because they are parents, they want to protect Shayla, too.*

Friends

Friends are your support system. They are the ones you turn to when you need advice, a shoulder to cry on, or a really good laugh. For your own peace of mind, it is important to maintain your friendships while you are in a romantic relationship. Falling in love can feel decidedly unsettling; friends offer safety and comfort. At some point, you may find yourself attracted to someone in your group of friends. This too can become complicated.

> *Since junior high there always has been this group of us. There's Tino, Rog, Becca, JoJo,*

Keith, Carlet, and me. That's the main bunch. Other people float in and out. Whenever somebody dates someone from the outside, then they're in . . . until they break up; then that person is outside again.

We meet up on the hill behind school in the morning or during lunch. We keep saying we're going to start a band, but no one knows how to play an instrument. Mostly we just talk and laugh at each other. Tino went out with Becca and I know he wanted to date Carlet back in eighth grade but she blew him off. She said she didn't want to ruin their friendship. Carlet had this boyfriend for a while last year. He hung out with her all the time and she brought him to the hill a lot. When they broke up, we all took her side and he didn't ever come back around.

We always say we'll be friends forever, but my brother says once you get out of high school things change. Maybe that's true, but I don't know what I'd do without my friends. They're always there to cheer me up or listen to me when things are bad. Even though sometimes I fight with them, I still care about them, and I know they care about me. That's what counts. That's why we're friends. Who else really knows me?

Starting a new romance can sometimes infringe on time spent with friends.

An important moment in a romantic relationship is introducing the person you love into the world in which you live—from your family to your friends. In turn, he or she will bring you into his or her world. A large part of falling in love involves taking chances, opening up to new experiences and people. You can learn a lot about each other when you hang out in each other's social circle.

Krista knew how important it was that the person she loved get along with her group of friends. "One guy I was hanging out with got in a fight with my best friend and that was a problem.

Starting a romantic relationship may mean spending less time with your friends. However, it is important to remember that your friends can be a source of emotional support.

I couldn't hang out with them together. It was a huge drag because I had to choose. It never worked. I would be with him wondering what my friends were doing. Then, if I was with my friends, I'd feel guilty and miss him. In the end, I chose my friends."

Friends might feel jealous or threatened when one of their own starts a romantic relationship. Friends often take up a large part of one's life, so spending a lot of time with someone new can cause friction. Friends may feel threatened, they may fear they are losing you. In some ways, that is true. Falling in love does bring about changes in a person's life. You may not have as much time to spend with your friends, but you can reassure them that they are an important and irreplaceable part of your life.

Sometimes you may not like or trust one of your new love's friends. This can cause friction in both your romantic relationships and your friendships. Try to talk things through; it is the best way to maintain your trust and love for each other. Starting a conversation that might be unpleasant is never appealing, but once you have cleared the air, you will feel like you have deepened your understanding of each other.

Talking Things Through

◎ Wait for your feelings to cool down so you can remain calm during the conversation.

◎ Choose a private place to talk.

◎ Choose a time when neither of you will be interrupted or distracted.

◎ Be patient and listen to what the other person is saying.

◎ Relate your feelings using phrases that begin with "I" instead of "you." In this way, you can avoid placing blame.

◎ Try not to end the conversation in anger.

Sex

Everyone appreciates the rhythm of falling in love. In *Rolling Stone* magazine, the Backstreet Boy's A. J. McLean revealed what he thinks is important in a romantic relationship. "It's really, really terrible how this world revolves around sex . . . people aren't focusing on the bigger, better issues, such as love, which is the kissing and the holding and the walking with hands together and the arms around each other—the more romantic things."

Although books and movies often equate sex with true love, every relationship is unique and each person in that relationship has different needs. Falling in love can be so overwhelming and special that you may find yourself drawn into a physical relationship. This can really complicate things.

Falling in love is intense, so it is best to proceed slowly. If the person you are involved with is trying to rush things, let him or her know how you feel, so that you both remain on the same emotional level. If the other person does not understand, then maybe you should rethink your relationship.

Romantic Gestures

Couples in love often feel like they are the only two people in the world and frequently find special ways to let each other know how much they care. Although

Holding hands while strolling down the street is one of many ways that lovers show affection for each other.

some couples prefer more traditional forms of showing affection, such as candy and flowers, there are limitless ways to express the love you feel—from instant e-mail messages to handwritten love notes.

Things That Can Make the Heart Flutter

◎ A special smile

◎ Your eyes meeting

◎ The touch of his or her hand

◎ The sound of his or her voice on the telephone

◎ Meaningful messages meant only for you

Certainly, some people are more expressive than others. There are the strong, silent types who let you know how they feel with just a look or a touch. Others may use grand gestures to sweep you off your feet. Still others may keep it all bottled up inside and then suddenly overwhelm you when you least expect it. As you explore romantic relationships, you will discover which expressions of love you are comfortable giving and receiving.

Chapter 4

Love Hurts

Sometimes love is a one-way street. You may meet someone you find attractive, only to be rejected. Love may also come too fast or serve as an escape from other negative situations, often resulting in stressful and unhealthy relationships. Even healthy relationships must weather possessiveness, jealousy, and heartache. The end of a long-term relationship can be excruciatingly painful.

When love hurts, you may feel as if you are the only person in the world ever to endure such pain. Friends and family can be sympathetic, most likely having felt the same way at some point in their lives. To some degree, you will have to learn to cope with feelings of rejection on your own, but you should think about

It often helps to talk to a friend when you feel rejected or when your romantic relationship has soured.

turning to friends or family for a shoulder to cry on and an ear to listen.

For most of tenth grade I liked this girl, Cindy. She didn't know it, but I'd gotten myself switched into her English class so I could see her every day. She was different from the kids that I hung around with. Her family had money. That's the way she acted, anyway. Not stuck-up or anything, but her clothes were nice and she carried herself differently.

I didn't think she noticed me much. There was this school dance at the end of the year, and I thought about asking her. I told some of my friends and they said that I should. I dressed up the day I was going to ask her. My friends gave me a hard time about that because it was the first time they'd seen me without jeans and sneakers. I thought, you know, if I was going to ask a girl like that out, I should look my best. I thought that then she'd think I was good enough to go out with.

It took me almost the whole day before I got up the nerve to ask her. A few of my friends said they'd talked to her about me and they thought she'd say yes. So I figured I might have a good chance, but I was still really nervous. When I finally asked her, she looked at me really sweet and told me that she was already going to the dance with somebody else. She smiled and said it was nice of me to ask her, though. I felt like such an idiot—all dressed up in those stupid clothes trying to be somebody I wasn't. I felt like a poser. I also felt like, even though she'd been nice and everything, that maybe that's just the way she was normally. She'd probably never really noticed me before, even though I'd been in love with her for about a year.

Unrequited Love

When you love someone who doesn't love you back, it's called unrequited love. It is deep and powerful, different

Realizing that someone you adore does not share your feelings can be painful.

from a crush because you may have been drawn to the person for a while and you may have a real desire to know him or her intimately. This kind of love can prove painful, especially when it becomes clear that the person you adore does not share your feelings. Once you have realized that the person you want does not want you, it may take some time to heal and eventually find someone who will return your affections.

Trusting Too Soon

As you begin to test the waters of love, it can be easy to mistake friendliness or flirting with a desire to start a relationship. As you become more comfortable with the person you are and what you have to offer, you will learn how to invite someone into your life gradually.

As you gain experience and wisdom, you may find that the less you try to make romance happen, the more likely it is to unfold.

Using Love to Escape

Sometimes falling in love seems like an easy escape from bad situations in the rest of your life. You may try to make love your security blanket. You may put up with behavior that would make you unhappy normally.

My friend Tamika has trouble believing she is loveable. When someone is into her, she feels so badly about herself that she latches on and fixates on the person and does not let go. It's really hard to watch because I care about her so much. The guys she goes out with don't treat her very well. They ignore her and insult her. When I point out that she doesn't have to deal with the way these guys treat her, she doesn't really hear me. I guess she has to figure out for herself how special she is.

Jealousy

For better or for worse, when you are in love, you may sometimes feel like a different person. Feelings of jealousy and possessiveness may rise inside when you least expect them.

Heather has a lot of guy friends. Recently, one of them was over at her house. Heather says, "Luke called up and said, 'I don't want him over at your house anymore.' I was furious because there was nothing going on and Luke knows how I feel about him. I would never hurt him. But I know he said it because he was afraid that I might like the guy. Plus, Luke lives far away. It can be difficult."

Arguments are a part of many relationships. Love can bring the highest highs, but it can also bring the lowest lows. Often arguments stem from feelings of sadness or insecurity. Rather than calmly explaining what is really going on in our hearts and minds, we sometimes lash out in anger or jealousy. Discuss these feelings with the person you love before you feel out of control.

Breaking Up

The loss of a love can bring not only heartbreak, but also unusual behavior. Some breakups are mutual. Others involve the outright rejection of one person by another. If you have been rejected, you may find yourself longing to see your former flame. You might walk by his or her house or visit places you used to frequent, hoping to run into him or her. You may obsess with worry that your lost love has found someone new.

After you have ended a relationship, you may find yourself longing for a lost love.

The person initiating the breakup may also struggle with conflicting emotions. Although this person may not feel rejected, he or she may experience guilt, relief, or doubt. He or she may second-guess the decision, wondering whether it was the right choice. He or she might fear being thought of as mean and cruel.

Ending a Relationship

◎ Have the conversation in person instead of over the telephone or via e-mail.

◎ Avoid assigning blame; instead try and explain your own feelings as clearly as you can.

◎ Try to get right to the point.

◎ Give each other some distance once you have broken up. If you share classes or programs, respect each other's space.

Memories

Regardless of who decides to end the relationship, recovering from the pain and sense of loss that accompany a breakup can feel like an endless journey. Knowing that time heals all wounds may seem like slim comfort at first, but eventually you will come to terms with the change. In fact, you may even realize that the experience has provided you with many fond memories you would not trade for the world.

After a relationship ends, doing things alone that you once enjoyed doing together might prove difficult at first. In time, though, as feelings of confusion and loss ease into acceptance, you may find that the experience has made you a stronger person. You may feel better prepared for relationships to come.

PCReservation Receipt

PC: COMPUTER 14

Date: 6/4/2007

Time: 11:55 AM

Length: 60 minutes

Location:

ADULT

can enjoy the fond
omantic relationship after
pain of a breakup.

The media's definitions of love engulf us—from songs to movies to commercials. It tells us what love is, how it is supposed to feel, and what products we need to purchase to attract it. Media messages can be amusing, confusing, annoying, comforting, and helpful. In fact, the sheer volume of these ideas can be overwhelming. When inundated with so many messages about love, it is important to remember that you are the one who chooses which, if any, of those words, sounds, and images have meaning.

Poetry and Music

Andreas explains his understanding of media, music, and love: "I think that love is a strong word and that today in society it is overused. The

media dishes out what they think people need and what they think people want to hear, and then they wait for it to be fed back to them. I think sometimes people are moved, but it has a lot to do with sex appeal, too.

"It's probably always been like that. I like it when an artist rises to the challenge of making a song interesting, because that's what love is supposed to be like . . . interesting. Music can overwhelm you with emotion. It has nothing to do with whether the person can sing or not, to me it's how he or she sings the song. Is the singer really feeling the heartbreak, the love?"

Although poems may seem like an old-fashioned way to let somebody know how you feel, the writing of poetry has long provided sweethearts with their most intimate moments. Love poetry can be breathtaking; it can also be downright corny. Whether written by a master poet or your first true love, a poem can movingly convey a message of love.

Writing about your feelings is also a very healthy personal outlet. Indeed, some people find it easier to write about, rather than talk about, their feelings. Writing, especially in a journal, is a great way to create a record of your experiences, enabling you to trace the way your perceptions of life and love have changed over time.

Many people find writing to or about the object of their affections a rewarding exercise.

The combination of poetry and music in a love song can transcend time and language. Music speaks to us on so many different levels. You can turn on the radio and hear a song that reminds you of a person you have loved and lost, or one that you still have in your heart. A song can take you back to a dark dance floor, a great flirtation, or the poignant memory of a first heartbreak.

As Alison explains, "Everything I know comes from music, both pain and pleasure. I think we create from pain. All of that anger can be channeled. The energies come out. I sing my best when I am angry and that's how I get it out of my system. The emotions can feel so strong that the song helps

*me with that sadness. Someone leaves you and it's
a song. Someone loves you and it's a song.*

Movies and Television

While music and poetry can seem like more intimate
and individual expressions of love, movies and television overtly express popular ideas about romance,
love, and relationships. Further, they reflect and
inform the social conventions of their era. In the 1970s,
Greg Brady kissed a girl at school on the *Brady Bunch,*
but viewers never saw it. Today, that small-screen kiss
happens in front of our eyes between Jack and Ethan
on *Dawson's Creek.*

Interestingly though, the overarching theme of love
and romance has remained a constant in popular stories
from centuries past all the way to the present. Many contemporary motion pictures are based on classic novels
and plays. For instance, Jane Austen's eighteenth-
century novel *Emma* inspired *Clueless.* The movie *Ten
Things I Hate About You* was based on Shakespeare's
sixteenth-century play *The Taming Of The Shrew.* The
popular attention both movies received speaks to our
enduring fascination with love.

The Beat Goes On

More often than not, it seems that the stories we read,
see, and hear about love are filled with drama or

Today, television shows, such as Dawson's Creek, *are more explicit in their depiction of romantic relationships.*

tragedy. Some have a happy ending. Many continue to chronicle the hero's search for his or her other half.

Falling in love may feel fantastic, but no one person can make you complete, only you can do that for yourself. Knowledge of the self and a belief in who you are form the basis of any solid and loving relationship. Bear in mind that no matter how many false starts and abrupt stops you endure on the road of love, you may find that when you least expect it, love will find its way to you in all of its wonderful incarnations.

Glossary

amphetamine   A stimulant affecting the central nervous system, that can be naturally released in the brain. It often works to speed up your heart.

Austen, Jane   A British writer who lived from 1775 to 1817. She is known for her penetrating observations of middle-class manners and morality, as well as her irony, wit, and style.

chivalry   The medieval actions that idealized knighthood, such as bravery, courtesy, honor, and gallantry toward women.

endorphins   A group of proteins that are found mainly in the brain. Endorphins reduce the sensation of pain and affect emotions.

heartbreak   Overwhelming sorrow, grief, or disappointment.

homophobia Irrational fear of, aversion to, or discrimination against homosexuals and homosexuality.

infatuation A short-lived passion for someone or something.

knight A soldier in medieval times. Usually born into wealth, knights often trained in the royal court.

minstrel A medieval entertainer who traveled from place to place, singing and reciting poetry.

myth A traditional, typically ancient story dealing with supernatural beings, ancestors, or heroes. These stories often reflect the ideals of that period's society.

neurochemistry The chemical composition of the nervous system.

Shakespeare, William An English playwright and poet who lived from 1564 to 1616 and who is considered one of the greatest writers in English literature.

For More Information

In the United States

National Coming Out Project
(800) 866-6263

Parents and Friends of Lesbians and Gays (PFLAG)
1726 M Street NW, Suite 400
Washington, DC 20036
(202) 467-8180
Web site: http://www.pflag.org

Planned Parenthood Federation of America
810 Seventh Avenue
New York, NY 10019
(800) 230-7526
(212) 541-7800
Web site: http://www.plannedparenthood.org

Teen Dating Intervention Project
2830 Massachusetts Avenue, Suite 101
Cambridge, MA 02141
(617) 354-2676

In Canada

Equality for Gays and Lesbians Everywhere (EGALE)
205-176 Glocester
Ottawa, ON K2P OA6
(613) 230-1043
Web site: http://www.egale.ca

Planned Parenthood Federation of Canada
1 Nicholas Street, Suite 430
Ottawa, ON K1N 7B7
(613) 241-4474
Web site: http://www.ppfc.ca

Web sites

iTurf
http://network.iturf.com

Miss Abigail's Time Warp Advice: Old Advice for
    Contemporary Dilemmas
http://www.missabigail.com

TeenOutReach.com
http://www.teenoutreach.com

For Further Reading

Bode, Janet. *Heartbreak and Roses: Real-Life Stories of Troubled Love*. Rev. ed. Danbury, CT: Franklin Watts, Inc., 2000.

Capellanus, Andreas. *The Art of Courtly Love*. New York: Columbia University Press, 1990.

Kass, Amy A., and Leon R. Kass, eds. *Wing to Wing, Oar to Oar: Readings on Courting and Marrying*. Notre Dame, IN: University of Notre Dame Press, 2000.

Kirberger, Kimberly, and Colin Mortensen. *A Journal on Relationships* (Teen Love Series). Deerfield Beach, FL: Health Communications, 1999.

Lindsay, Jeanne Warren. *Teenage Couples: Caring, Commitment, and Change: How to Build a Relationship That Lasts*. Buena Park, CA: Morning Glory Press, 1995.

Neruda, Pablo. *Twenty Love Poems and a Song Of Despair*. San Francisco: Chronicle Books, 1993.

Ross, Stanley. *The Meaning of Courtly Love*. Albany, NY: State University Press, 1969.

Shakespeare, William. *Romeo and Juliet*. New York: Oxford University Press, 2000.

Shakespeare, William. *The Sonnets: Poems of Love*. New York: St. Martin's Press, 1980.

Youngs, Bettie B. *Taste Berries for Teens: Inspirational Short Stories and Encouragement on Life, Love, Friendship and Tough Issues*. Deerfield Beach, FL: Health Communications, 1999.

Index

About the Author

Lauren Spencer is originally from California and now lives in New York City, where she teaches writing workshops in the public schools. She also writes lifestyle and music articles for magazines.

Photo Credits

Cover and pp. 2, 34, 37, 46 by Maura Boruchow; pp. 7, 14, 16, 21, 56 © The Everett Collection; p. 11 ©Araldo de Luca/Corbis; p. 18 © Corbis; pp. 20, 23, 26, 33, 41, 49, 51, 54 by Sara Kunstler; p. 28 © Reuters NewMedia Inc./Corbis; p. 30 © N. Richmond/The Image Works; p. 38 © Bob Daemmrich Photos/The Image Works; p. 44 © Skjold Stock.

Series Design

Tom Forget

Layout

Claudia Carlson

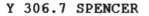